MW00713966

CHANGING LANDSCAPES
BY MARIA GILL

INTRODUCTION

Imagine you go back in time thousands of years. You are in a place that you have never seen before. But it's where you live now. The **landscape** has changed. The mountains are taller. Rivers run through the land. Why does the landscape look so different?

Water made this canyon.

Huge waves can change the landscape.

Some changes to the landscape take thousands of years. Mountains slowly wear away. Rivers become wider.

Other changes to the landscape **happen** quickly. Natural disasters like hurricanes or earthquakes can **alter** the landscape **suddenly**.

3

CHAPTER 1

SLOW CHANGES

Water can make big changes to the landscape.

Rivers and streams shape the landscape. The water in rivers and streams carries **sediment**, or small rocks and sand. The **movement** of the rock and sand is called **erosion**.

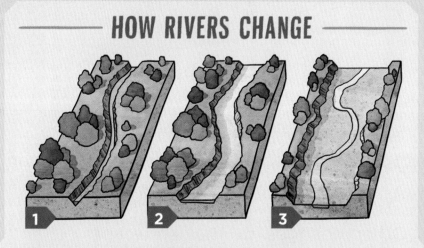

HOW RIVERS CHANGE

1. A river cuts a path through the land.
2. Over time, the river wears away more land.
3. The river leaves behind rocks and sand, and a flat plain forms.

Erosion wore away these cliffs.

The water from waves can remove sand from beaches. Waves can also wear away cliffs. Waves slowly break rocks into smaller pieces. This is called **weathering**.

The wind also causes erosion. Wind blows the sand. The sand forms hills called dunes.

STOP AND CHECK

How does water change the landscape?

Sometimes natural **features**, such as sand dunes, protect the land from erosion.

Sand dunes act as barriers. They trap the sand brought by the wind and waves. Grasses keep the sand from blowing away.

Wetlands slow down erosion. Wetlands are marshes or swamps. They are found near rivers, lakes, or oceans. Wetlands absorb, or soak up, water when it rains. This prevents flooding from happening.

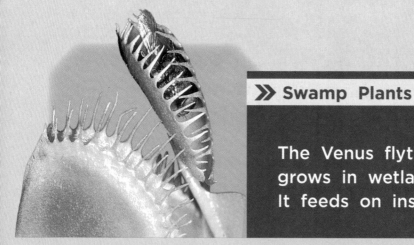

》Swamp Plants

The Venus flytrap grows in wetlands. It feeds on insects.

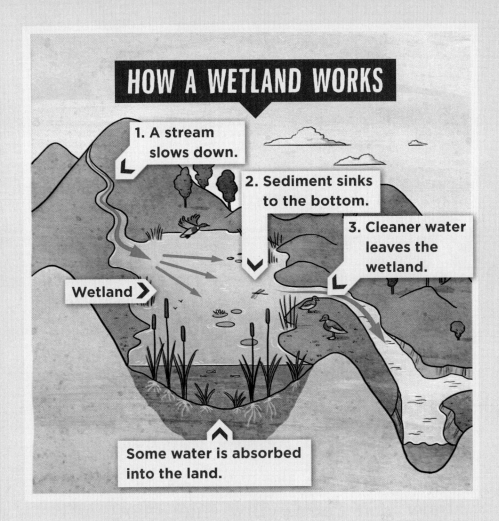

The roots of a wetland plant hold the soil in place. This helps prevent erosion.

STOP AND CHECK

How do wetlands prevent erosion?

CHAPTER 2

SUDDEN CHANGES!

A landslide hit this town in California.

Natural disasters change the land more quickly than erosion.

One kind of natural disaster is a landslide. It is **unpredictable**. This means that it can happen without warning. Heavy rain causes landslides. The ground becomes filled with water. It can't absorb any more. Rocks and soil slide downhill. Sometimes the hillside **collapses**.

Landslides move very quickly. They can bury towns and roads.

Trees and plants help prevent landslides. The roots of trees and plants keep the soil in place. The roots absorb water. Landslides are less likely to happen on hillsides with trees and plants.

Hurricanes can also change the landscape. Hurricanes are **severe** storms that begin in the ocean. When a hurricane nears land, the wind makes huge waves. These waves wash away the sand from beaches. That can make the beach much smaller.

Hurricane Katrina caused a lot of damage.

Wetlands protect areas from hurricanes. The wetlands absorb some of the water from the rain and waves.

STOP AND CHECK

What damage do hurricanes cause?

» **Hurricane Katrina**

In 2005, Hurricane Katrina hit the Gulf Coast and caused a crisis. Strong winds and rain caused a lot of damage. Many areas were flooded.

CHAPTER 3

FIXING THE DAMAGE

People can also cause erosion. They cut down trees to build roads or houses. Trees protect against erosion. Their roots absorb water. They keep the soil from washing away in heavy rain. They prevent **hazards** such as landslides.

Trees and plants with deep roots help prevent landslides.

People can **restore** wetlands and dunes. This can prevent erosion. They can stop building on wetlands. They can plant more wetlands.

Gull on spill Aaron Nueth Photography

STOP AND CHECK

How can people stop erosion?

Restoring wetlands prevents erosion.

13

CONCLUSION

Imagine you have gone back in time again. You have seen the changes to mountains, rivers, and coasts. These changes happen very slowly.

You have seen sudden changes caused by natural disasters. We can't stop disasters from happening but we can try to prevent some of the damage they cause.

A student plants grasses at a wetland.

7/IMA Press/Newscom

Respond to Reading

Summarize

How does the landscape change over time? Use your graphic organizer to help you summarize.

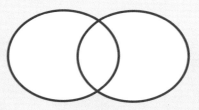

Text Evidence

1. Reread Chapter 2. What is the same about landslides and hurricanes? What is different? COMPARE AND CONTRAST

2. What is the meaning of *quickly* on page 3? Which words help you figure out the meaning? VOCABULARY

3. Write about how changes to the landscape from erosion or a natural disaster are similar. Write about how they are different. WRITE ABOUT READING

Compare Texts
Read about how some students are helping to prevent erosion.

Students Save Wetlands

People in Florida are saving wetlands. Wetlands were damaged when houses and buildings were built.

Wetlands help prevent **destruction** from floods. They prevent erosion.

The students are restoring wetlands. They are planting grasses. The grasses will hold the soil in place.

How to Grow Wetland Grasses

1. The students plant grasses in a pond.

2. They check on the grasses. They test the water.

3. The students wait six to eight months. Then they dig up the grasses. They replant them and give them more room to grow.

4. When the grasses finish growing, the students plant them in a wetland.

17

The grasses the students have planted will provide homes for birds and fish. The grasses will stop erosion.

The students have made a **substantial** difference. They planted almost 24 acres of wetlands on the Florida coast.

Restoring the wetlands provides homes for birds like the white ibis.

Tim Laman/National Geographic/Getty Images

Make Connections

Why is it important to plant new wetlands?

ESSENTIAL QUESTION

How do people in *Changing Landscapes* and *Students Save Wetlands* prevent erosion?

TEXT TO TEXT

Glossary

erosion *(i-ROH-zhuhn)* the wearing away of land by wind or water *(page 4)*

sediment *(SED-uh-muhnt)* rocks and sand moved by water or wind *(page 4)*

weathering *(WETH-uhr-ing)* slow damage to rocks *(page 5)*

wetlands *(WET-landz)* areas of land that stay wet *(page 6)*

Index

Focus on Science

Purpose To understand the damage a natural disaster can cause and how to get ready for one

Procedure

Step 1 Choose a natural disaster you want to learn about.

Step 2 Find out what damage this disaster causes. Use the library or the Internet.

Step 3 Find out how people can get ready for this kind of disaster, such as making an emergency kit.

Step 4 Make a poster. List the facts you learned about the disaster. Make sure you say what the disaster is. You also need to say what dangers it creates and how people can stay safe.

Conclusion Getting ready helps us to stay safe. What have you learned about planning for a natural disaster?